A Note From Rick Renner

I am on a personal quest to see a "revival of the Bible" so people can establish their lives on a firm foundation that will stand strong and endure the test as end-time storm winds begin to intensify.

In order to experience a revival of the Bible in your personal life, it is important to take time each day to read, receive, and apply its truths to your life. James tells us that if we will continue in the perfect law of liberty — refusing to be forgetful hearers, but determined to be doers — we will be blessed in our ways. As you watch or listen to the programs in this series and work through this corresponding study guide, I trust you will search the Scriptures and allow the Holy Spirit to help you hear something new from God's Word that applies specifically to your life. I encourage you to be a doer of the Word He reveals to you. Whatever the cost, I assure you — it will be worth it.

> Thy words were found, and I did eat them;
> and thy word was unto me the joy and rejoicing of mine heart:
> for I am called by thy name, O Lord God of hosts.
> — Jeremiah 15:16

Your brother and friend in Jesus Christ,

Rick Renner

Unless otherwise indicated, all scripture quotations are taken from the *King James Version* of the Bible.

Scripture quotations marked (*AMPC*) are taken from the *Amplified® Bible, Classic Edition*. Copyright © 1954, 1958, 1962, 1964, 1965, 1987 by The Lockman Foundation. Used by permission. www.Lockman.org.

Scripture quotations marked (*NKJV*) are taken from the *New King James Version®*. Copyright © 1982 by Thomas Nelson. Used by permission. All rights reserved.

Do You Want To Be Healed?

Copyright © 2019 by Rick Renner
1814 W. Tacoma St.
Broken Arrow, OK 74012-1406

Published by Rick Renner Ministries
www.renner.org

ISBN 13: 978-1-6803-1606-3

ISBN 13 eBook: 978-1-6803-1644-5

All rights reserved. No portion of this book may be reproduced or transmitted in any form or by any means — electronic, mechanical, photocopy, recording, scanning, or other — except for brief quotations in critical reviews or articles, without the prior written permission of the Publisher.

How To Use This Study Guide

This five-lesson study guide corresponds to *"Do You Want To Be Healed?" With Rick Renner* (Renner TV). Each lesson in this study guide covers a topic that is addressed during the program series, with questions and references supplied to draw you deeper into your own private study of the Scriptures on this subject.

To derive the most benefit from this study guide, consider the following:

First, watch or listen to the program prior to working through the corresponding lesson in this guide. (Programs can also be viewed at **renner.org** by clicking on the Media/Archives links or on our Renner Ministries YouTube channel.)

Second, take the time to look up the scriptures included in each lesson. Prayerfully consider their application to your own life.

Third, use a journal or notebook to make note of your answers to each lesson's Study Questions and Practical Application challenges.

Fourth, invest specific time in prayer and in the Word of God to consult with the Holy Spirit. Write down the scriptures or insights He reveals to you.

Finally, take action! Whatever the Lord tells you to do according to His Word, do it.

For added insights on this subject, it is recommended that you obtain Rick Renner's book *You Can Get Over It*. You may also select from Rick's other available resources by placing your order at **renner.org** or by calling 1-800-742-5593.

LESSON 1

TOPIC
The Pool of Bethesda

SCRIPTURES
1. **John 5:1-4** — After this there was a feast of the Jews; and Jesus went up to Jerusalem. Now there is at Jerusalem by the sheep market a pool, which is called in the Hebrew tongue Bethesda, having five porches. In these lay a great multitude of impotent folk, of blind, halt, withered, waiting for the moving of the water. For an angel went down at a certain season into the pool, and troubled the water: whosoever then first after the troubling of the water stepped in was made whole of whatsoever disease he had.

GREEK WORDS
1. "sheep market" — προβατικῇ (*probatike*): pictures a sheep gate; a gate where sheep were kept or sold for temple sacrifices, and it was only a short distance from the temple
2. "pool" — κολυμβήθρα (*kolumbethra*): a pool; a highly sophisticated, beautifully developed place
3. "Bethesda" — Βηθζαθά (*Bethzatha*): a house of mercy; a house of grace; a house of goodness
4. "porches" — στοὰς (*stoas*): covered porches; covered porticoes; covered colonnades
5. "lay" — κατάκειμαι (*katakeimai*): to lie down; pictures things that are piled around
6. "great multitude" — πλῆθος (*plethos*): a great number; a multitude
7. "impotent folk" — ἀσθενέω (*astheneo*): describes a person who is frail in health; one so physically weak that he is unable to travel; one who is feeble, fragile, faint, incapacitated, disabled, or simply in such poor health that it would be unthinkable to transport him; shut in or homebound; can also mean to be in financial need
8. "blind" — τυφλός (*tuphlos*): blind, physically or mentally
9. "halt" — χωλός (*cholos*): maimed; deprived of limbs; crippled

10. "withered" — ξηρός (*xeros*): deprived of natural strength; pictures those whose physical limbs are shrunk, wasted, or withered away
11. "waiting" — ἐκδέχομαι (*ekdechomai*): from ἐκ (*ek*), meaning *out*, and δέχομαι (*dechomai*)
12. meaning *welcome*; to welcome; to await; to fully expect; to anticipate; pictures looking to the end result or outcome of the waiting; full expectation and anticipation
13. "moving" — κίνησις (*kenesis*): stirring; commotion; agitation; fierce moving
14. "went down" — καταβαίνω (*katabaino*): to descend, like stepping down a set of stairs
15. "troubled" — ταράσσω (*tarasso*): to disturb; to distress; to panic; to deeply trouble; to trouble back and forth; to be deeply disturbed
16. "stepped in" — ἐμβαίνω (*embaino*): to step in, as to step into a pool
17. "whole" — ὑγιής (*hugies*): healthy; sound; well; whole; fully restored to normal health
18. "disease" — νόσος (*nosos*): a terminal condition for which there is no natural cure; in the ancient world, it especially described spirit-induced illnesses; this type of disease held no hope of recuperation; an unalterable, irreversible, incurable condition
19. "had" — ἔχω (*echo*): tense meaning *having*; also, to be in the embrace of; suppressed; restrained

SYNOPSIS

The five lessons in this study entitled ***Do You Want To Be Healed?*** will focus on the following topics:

- The Pool of Bethesda
- Everything Changes When Jesus Enters the Picture
- The Question That Will Change Your Life
- The Ramifications of Total Healing in Your Life
- What if Others Don't Rejoice When You Change?

The emphasis of this lesson:

The Pool of Bethesda was a beautifully developed place where a multitude of people with incurable diseases waited in faith for God's mercy and goodness to be graciously poured out in the form of healing.

For 38 years, a man lay lame at the Pool of Bethesda, waiting for his opportunity to receive supernatural healing. Month after month and year after year, he watched as others were miraculously made whole, yet he never experienced the restorative power of God for which he longed. Prolonged delay turned into discouragement and depression. Into this scene, Jesus — the Great Physician — entered. When He saw this man, He healed him by the power of His Word, and He is still healing and transforming lives today!

Entering Jerusalem

As one journeys toward Jerusalem coming from the east, he can enter the old city through what is called the "Lions' Gate." Centuries earlier, this entrance was called "Stephen's Gate," as it was the location where Stephen, one of the first disciples of Jesus, was martyred for his faith (*see* Acts 7). Once through the Lions' Gate, the Via Dolorosa begins, which was road upon which Jesus made His final walk on His way to Golgotha — the place of His crucifixion.

Shortly after one begins this path, he can see Church of St. Anne to the right. It was built by the Crusaders in the Twelfth Century, and the reason for its construction was to honor someone significant. In the basement of this church are the remains of a First Century house that is believed to have been the birthplace of Anne, the mother of the Virgin Mary. Whether this is accurate or not, we do not know. If it is true, it presents a good reason why Jesus would be in this area the day he went to the Pool of Bethesda, which is located nearby. It is possible He was visiting His grandparents that day!

As one continues his walk north-northwestward, he arrives at what was called the "Sheep Gate"— the same gate Jesus went through as recorded in John 5. The Bible says, "After this there was a feast of the Jews; and Jesus went up to Jerusalem. Now there is at Jerusalem by the sheep market a pool, which is called in the Hebrew tongue Bethesda, having five porches" (John 5:1,2).

The words "sheep market" in verse 2 are actually referring to the "sheep gate." It is translated from the Greek word *probatike*, and it describes *a sheep gate; a gate where sheep were kept or sold for temple sacrifices*. It was only a short distance from the temple. Once Jesus walked through the sheep gate, He came upon the Pool of Bethesda — a place of great anticipation for the healing power of God to be released.

The Place Called Bethesda

The Pool of Bethesda was quite a remarkable place. John 5:2 says, "Now there is at Jerusalem by the sheep market a pool, which is called in the Hebrew tongue Bethesda, having five porches." The word "pool" is the Greek word *kolumbethra*, and it describes *a pool that was highly sophisticated and beautiful; a magnificently developed place*. It is the same word used to describe the Pool of Siloam (*see* John 9), which was also very luxurious and magnificent.

Bethesda wasn't a muddy, dirty pond. It was a highly developed location originally built for and occupied by wealthy, educated, cultured, and affluent people; they were the intelligentsia of the day. But for various reasons, they abandoned it, and it began to be occupied by a host of sick people. Interestingly, "Bethesda" was not its original name. The sick who took over the place renamed it Bethesda, for good reason.

The word "Bethesda" is the Greek word *Bethzatha*, which means *a house of mercy; a house of grace; a house of goodness*. Clearly, Bethesda was a place where God's mercy was poured out. He graciously performed merciful acts on the sick, making His goodness known to them and to all who looked on.

The Sick Lay Under Five Porches

The Bible says there were five "porches" at Bethesda. The word "porches" is the Greek word *stoas*, which describes *long covered porches; covered porticoes; covered colonnades*. These walkways were usually decorated with magnificent frescos (murals), beautifully hand-carved columns, and a roof that was overlaid in tile. These five *stoas* (porches) were huge and housed many who were sick.

Verse 3 says, "In these lay a great multitude of impotent folk, of blind, halt, withered, waiting for the moving of the water." Notice it says the sick "lay" under these porches. The Greek word for "lay" is *katakeimai*, which is the compound of two words: *kata*, which means *down*, and the word *keimai*, which means *to lay*. When the two words are compounded to form *katakeimai*, it means *to lie down*, and it pictures *things that are piled around*.

The word *katakeimai* is the same word used in Matthew 8:14 to describe Peter's mother-in-law, who "lay" sick with fever. She had been down and out of commission for quite some time until Jesus came and healed her. The Bible says that at Bethesda there was "a great multitude" lying there. The phrase "great multitude" is the Greek word *plethos*, which describes *a great number, a multitude*. In other words, the "porches" (*stoas*) were densely populated with sick people. In fact, there were so many sick people, they looked like "sardines in a can" — one person next to another to another, etc.

They Had Various Sicknesses

John 5:3 describes the multitude of sick people as "impotent folk," which is the Greek word *astheneo*. It describes *a person who is frail in health; one so physically weak that he is unable to travel; one who is feeble, fragile, faint, incapacitated, disabled, or simply in such poor health that it would be unthinkable to transport him*. It also refers to one who is *shut in or homebound* or *one in financial need*. The words "impotent folk" paint a profound picture of sickness in that these people had spent all their money on medical help, yet hadn't gotten any better.

The Bible goes on to say that there were "blind" people at Bethesda. The word "blind" is the Greek word *tuphlos*, which describes *those who are blind, physically or mentally*. As a rule, blindness was incurable. At that time, it was believed that if you could heal a blind person, you were endowed with great power.

The "halt" were also present at Bethesda. The Greek word for "halt" is *cholos*, and it describes *the maimed; those deprived of limbs; the crippled*. In some way, these people had been severely physically afflicted.

The "withered" were also among the crowd. The word "withered" in the Greek is *xeros*, which means *deprived of their natural strength*. Their physical limbs are shrunk, wasted, or withered away. This is actually where we get the word *zero*. In the eyes of society, the "withered" were *zeros* — they had nothing worthwhile offer.

They Were Waiting for the Water's Moving

All these impotent folk — the blind, the halt, and the withered — were lying beneath five porches at the Pool of Bethesda *waiting* for the moving of the water. The word "waiting" is the Greek word *ekdechomai*, which is from the word *ek*, meaning *out*, and *dechomai*, meaning *welcome; to welcome; to await; to fully expect; to anticipate*. It pictures looking to the end result or outcome of the waiting with *full expectation* and *anticipation*.

With great anticipation, the people's eyes were fixed on the water waiting for it to begin moving. The word "moving" is the Greek word *kenesis*, and it describes *a stirring; commotion; agitation; or fierce moving*. This word *kenesis* doesn't describe the natural movement of the water. This *kenesis* was likely a circular rotation for which there was no natural explanation.

The cause was supernatural. John 5:4 says, "For an angel went down at a certain season into the pool, and troubled the water: whosoever then first after the troubling of the water stepped in was made whole of whatsoever disease he had." The phrase "went down" is the Greek word *katabaino*, which means *to descend, like stepping down a set of stairs*. Thus, the angel descended from Heaven and into the pool like he was walking down a set of stairs.

Once the angel was in the water, he "troubled" it, which is the Greek word *tarasso*, meaning *to disturb; to distress; to panic; to deeply trouble; to trouble back and forth; to be deeply disturbed*. As with the word "moving" (*kenesis*), there was nothing natural about this back-and-forth motion. It was supernatural. And the first one to step into the pool when the water was "troubled" was made "whole." In Greek, the word "whole" is *hugies*, meaning *healthy; sound; well; whole; fully restored to normal health*.

Regardless of the disease a person had, full restoration and soundness were experienced when he stepped into the pool in faith. The word "disease" is the Greek word *nosos*, and it describes *a terminal condition for which there is no natural cure*. In the ancient world, it especially described *spirit-induced illnesses*. This type of disease held no hope of recuperation; it was an unalterable, irreversible, incurable condition.

Thus, these people with incurable diseases waited with great anticipation for the miraculous movement of the water at Bethesda — the moment God's mercy was manifested. Just as He sent the angel to trouble the water then, He is stirring up the atmosphere around you now. His healing is available to you, regardless of the severity of your ailment.

STUDY QUESTIONS

> Study to shew thyself approved unto God, a workman that needeth not to be ashamed, rightly dividing the word of truth.
> — 2 Timothy 2:15

1. The historical facts surrounding the Pool of Bethesda are fascinating. What new insights have you learned about this amazing place of healing in Jesus' day?
2. According to Exodus 15:26, Psalm 103:1-3, and Acts 10:38, how important do you think physical healing is to God? What do these notable passages speak to you?

PRACTICAL APPLICATION

> But be ye doers of the word, and not hearers only, deceiving your own selves.
> — James 1:22

Imagine you were the man at the Pool of Bethesda. For 38 years, you had been waiting for your moment to be the first one to step into the water when the angel supernaturally stirred it up.

1. What kinds of thoughts might have been going through your mind?
2. What types of feelings might you have felt after waiting all those years?
3. What do you think motivated this man to move to Bethesda in the first place?

LESSON 2

TOPIC
Everything Changes When Jesus Enters the Picture

SCRIPTURES

1. **John 5:1-6** — After this there was a feast of the Jews; and Jesus went up to Jerusalem. Now there is at Jerusalem by the sheep market a pool, which is called in the Hebrew tongue Bethesda, having five porches. In these lay a great multitude of impotent folk, of blind, halt, withered, waiting for the moving of the water. For an angel went down at a certain season into the pool, and troubled the water: whosoever then first after the troubling of the water stepped in was made whole of whatsoever disease he had. And a certain man was there, which had an infirmity thirty and eight years. When Jesus saw him lie, and knew that he had been now a long time in that case, he saith unto him, Wilt thou be made whole?

GREEK WORDS

1. "sheep market" — προβατικῇ (*probatike*): pictures a sheep gate; a gate where sheep were kept or sold for temple sacrifices, and it was only a short distance from the temple

2. "pool" — κολυμβήθρα (*kolumbethra*): a pool; a highly sophisticated, beautiful, developed place

3. "Bethesda" — Βηθζαθά (*Bethzatha*): a house of mercy; a house of grace; a house of goodness

4. "porches" — στοὰς (*stoas*): covered porches; covered porticoes; covered colonnades

5. "lay" — κατάκειμαι (*katakeimai*): to lie down; pictures things that are piled around

6. "great multitude" — πλῆθος (*plethos*): a great number; a multitude

7. "impotent folk" — ἀσθενέω (*astheneo*): describes a person who is frail in health; one so physically weak that he is unable to travel; one who is feeble, fragile, faint, incapacitated, disabled, or simply in such

Do You Want To Be Healed? | 11

poor health that it would be unthinkable to transport him; shut-in or homebound; can also mean to be in financial need

8. "blind" — τυφλός (*tuphlos*): blind, physically or mentally
9. "halt" — χωλός (*cholos*): maimed; deprived of limbs; crippled
10. "withered" — ξηρός (*xeros*): deprived of natural strength; pictures those whose physical limbs are shrunk, wasted, or withered away
11. "waiting" — ἐκδέχομαι (*ekdechomai*): from ἐκ (*ek*), meaning out, and δέχομαι (*dechomai*), meaning *welcome*; to welcome; to await; to fully expect; to anticipate; pictures looking to the end result or outcome of the waiting; full expectation and anticipation
12. "moving" — κίνησις (*kenesis*): stirring; commotion; agitation; fierce moving
13. "went down" — καταβαίνω (*katabaino*): to descend, like stepping down a set of stairs
14. "troubled" — ταράσσω (*tarasso*): to disturb; to distress; to panic; to deeply trouble; to trouble back and forth; to be deeply disturbed
15. "stepped in" — ἐμβαίνω (*embaino*): to step in, as to step into a pool
16. "whole" — ὑγιής (*hugies*): healthy; sound; well; whole; fully restored to normal health
17. "disease" — νόσος (*nosos*): a terminal condition for which there is no natural cure; in the ancient world, it especially described spirit-induced illnesses; this type of disease held no hope of recuperation; an unalterable, irreversible, incurable condition
18. "had" — ἔχω (*echo*): tense meaning having; also, to be in the embrace of; suppressed; restrained
19. "certain" — τις (*tis*): certain; specific; notable
20. "infirmity" — ἀσθενεία (*astheneia*): describes a person who is frail in health; one so physically weak that he is unable to travel; one who is feeble, fragile, faint, incapacitated, disabled, or simply in such poor health that it would be unthinkable to transport him; shut in or homebound; can also mean to be in financial need
21. "saw" — ὁράω (*horao*): to see; to behold; to perceive; pictures a scrutinizing look; to look with the intent to examine; to fully view; to experience; to know from personal observation
22. "lie" — κατάκειμαι (*katakeimai*): in context, pictures one who is very sick; lying down; down and out

23. "knew" — γινώσκω (*ginosko*): to know, perceive, or comprehend; to recognize a person or a thing; to acknowledge; to have a full comprehension about a person or thing
24. "had" — ἔχω (*echo*): tense meaning having; also, to be in the embrace of; suppressed; restrained
25. "long time" — πολὺν ἤδη χρόνον (*polun ede chronon*): a long time already in this chronic condition
26. "wilt thou" — Θέλεις (Theleis): a form of θέλω (*thelo*), conveying desire, wish, will, or intention

SYNOPSIS

The Pool of Bethesda was a sought-after place by numerous people with incurable diseases. This spring-fed pool was located in Jerusalem near the Sheep Gate and the Tower of Antonia. It was here that the people believed the power of God periodically showed up to heal the sick — and it is where Jesus found a man who had been waiting for 38 years to receive his healing.

The emphasis of this lesson:

Bethesda boasted of five highly-decorated porches, and under them lay the blind, halt, withered, and impotent folk. All had faith that they could be healed when the water was supernaturally stirred — including one man who had been there 38 years.

Where Was Bethesda Located?

John 5:1 and 2 tells us where the Pool of Bethesda can be found. Verse 1 says, "…There was a feast of the Jews; and Jesus went up to Jerusalem." Jesus honored the holy days established by God through Moses. That is what brought Him to Jerusalem at that time. Verse 2 says, "Now there is at Jerusalem by the sheep market a pool, which is called in the Hebrew tongue Bethesda, having five porches."

The words "sheep market" are from the Greek word *probatike*, which pictures *a sheep gate; a gate where sheep were kept or sold for temple sacrifices.* This sheep gate was only a short distance from the temple. The Sheep Gate, which is still in existence today, was located in a remote area of Jerusalem near the backside of the temple. Entering the city from the Mount of Olives today, one would pass through what is called the "Lions' Gate." It was given this name because of the lions that are carved in stone above the entrance. Centuries earlier, this gate was called "Stephen's Gate," as it was believed by the Early Church fathers to be the location where the disciple Stephen was stoned to death for his faith in Christ (*see* Acts 7).

After walking through the Lions' Gate, one would immediately find himself on the Via Dolorosa, which means *the way of suffering*. It was the path Jesus walked when He carried His cross to Golgotha. On the right, a traveler would see an ancient church built as late as the Twelfth Century by the Crusaders. It is the Church of St. Anne, and it is named after Anne, the mother of the Virgin Mary. A staircase inside the church takes you down to the remains of a First Century house that is believed to be where Mary's mother was born.

If this actually was the house were Jesus' grandparents lived, it offers good reason for Jesus' being in the vicinity the day He visited the Pool of Bethesda. The Sheep Gate, translated as *sheep market* in the King James Bible, was very close to Bethesda, which is what we see in John 5:2.

What Was Bethesda Like?

John 5:2 says, "Now there is at Jerusalem by the sheep market a pool, which is called in the Hebrew tongue Bethesda, having five porches." The word "Bethesda" in Greek is the word *Bethzatha*, and it means *a house of mercy; a house of grace; a house of goodness*. Bethesda was a place where God's presence showed up and His mercy, grace, and goodness were poured out on the sick.

Notice the phrase "which is called." This actually means *which has been nicknamed or renamed or is being called by others as*. This lets us know that Bethesda was not the original name given to this place. It is the name the sick people gave it after they took ownership.

Initially, the Pool of Bethesda was created for and was occupied by the intelligentsia of the day — the affluent, the highly educated, and the wealthy. We know this to be true because of the use of the word "pool" — the Greek word *kolumbethra*. It describes *a pool that is highly sophisticated and luxurious; a beautiful, developed place*. It is the same word used to describe the Pool of Siloam, which was also an enormous place of opulence.

Bethesda Had Five Porches

The Bible states that Bethesda had five "porches." As we learned in our first lesson, the word "porches" is the Greek word *stoas*. It is a familiar term used throughout both the Greek and Roman world, and it describes *long covered porches*; *covered porticoes*; or *covered colonnades*. These roofed walkways normally featured beautiful mosaics and were supported by magnificent hand-carved columns. These *stoas* were everywhere, including in the cities of Rome, Athens, Sparta, and Smyrna.

The fact that there were five *stoas* at the Pool of Bethesda indicates that an enormous amount of money had been invested there. Excavations reveal that there were actually two pools at Bethesda — a lower pool, which was 55 feet long, and an upper pool measuring 60 feet in length. It was the upper pool that had the five covered porches (*stoas*).

It was under these five covered porticoes that there "…lay a great multitude of impotent folk, of blind, halt, withered, waiting for the moving of the water" (John 5:3). The word "lay" is the Greek word *katakeimai*, which means *to lie down*. This word pictures *things that are piled around*. The word *katakeimai* can also be translated as *incapacitated* or *disabled*. The people that lay at Bethesda were incapacitated and unable to normally function.

How many were there at this pool? Scripture says a "great multitude" — the Greek word *plethos*, meaning *a great number*, *a multitude*. If you would have peeked in on Bethesda, you would have seen sick people packed around this pool like sardines crammed in a can. There was one sick person alongside another sick person *alongside another sick person*.

Who Was Lying Under the Porches?

The Bible says there was a great multitude of "impotent folk," which is the Greek word *astheneo*, and it describes *a person who is frail in health*; *one so physically weak that he is unable to travel*; *one who is feeble, fragile, faint, incapacitated, disabled, or simply in such poor health that it would be unthinkable to transport him*. It can also indicate *one who is shut in or homebound* or *people who are in financial need*.

If we stop to really think about it, we realize that sickness is a monstrous, evil thief. It steals your time, your attention, your peace, your joy, and your finances. It will leave you in dire straits on many levels.

The "blind" were also under these five porches. The Greek word for "blind" is *tuphlos*, meaning *blind, physically or mentally*. The "halt" were there, too, which is the word *cholos* in Greek, and it denotes *those who are physically maimed, deprived of limbs, or crippled*.

A third category of people at the Pool of Bethesda were the "withered." This is the Greek word *xeros*, which is from where we get the word *zero*. It means *deprived of natural strength*, and it pictures those *whose physical limbs are shrunk, wasted, or withered away*. As far as society was concerned, the sick people at Bethesda were the big "zeros" in life.

They Were Waiting for the Moving of the Water

There they were — the blind, halt, withered, and impotent folk — all gathered under the porches at Bethesda, "waiting for the moving of the water" (vs. 3). The word "waiting" is the Greek word *ekdechomai*. It is taken from *ek*, meaning *out*, and *dechomai*, which means *welcome; to welcome; to await; to fully expect; to anticipate*. It pictures *looking to the end result or outcome of the waiting; anticipation and full expectation*.

Essentially, those who were sick at Bethesda had their eyes focused on the water, and they didn't look away from it. They were waiting for its "moving." The word "moving" is the Greek word *kenesis*, and it describes *a stirring; commotion; agitation;* or *fierce moving*. This was not a natural movement of water, but a supernatural movement.

John 5:4 reveals what produced this supernatural movement. It says, "For an angel went down at a certain season into the pool, and troubled the water…." The phrase "went down" is the Greek word *katabaino*, and it means *to descend, like stepping down a set of stairs*. The angel came down and descended into the pool like one who descends a staircase.

Once the angel was in the pool, he "troubled the water." This word "troubled" in Greek is *tarasso*, and it means *to disturb; to distress; to panic; to deeply trouble; to trouble back and forth; to be deeply disturbed*. Essentially, the water was in a state of panic. It began moving fiercely in a circular motion, and that was the signal that God's mercy and goodness were available.

They Believed They Would Be Made Whole

Verse 4 goes on to say, "…Whosoever then first after the troubling of the water stepped in was made whole…." The people believed that the first person to step in after the water was troubled would be made "whole." The Greek word for "whole" is *hugies*, and it describes *one who is healthy; sound; well; whole; fully restored to normal health*.

The sick around the Pool of Bethesda had faith that they would be totally cured of "whatsoever disease he had." The word "disease" is the Greek word *nosos*, and it describes *a terminal condition for which there is no natural cure*. In the ancient world, it especially described *spirit-induced illnesses*. This type of disease held no hope of recuperation. It was *an unalterable, irreversible, incurable condition*.

Interestingly, the word "had" is also important. It is the Greek word *echo*, and its tense carries the meaning *having*. It can also mean *to be in the embrace of; suppressed; or restrained*. In other words, the lives of those who were sick had been suppressed and restrained by their affliction. Sickness had stopped them from being and doing what they wanted to be and do.

One Man Was Held Captive Thirty-Eight Years

One man in particular had been suppressed and restrained for nearly four decades. John 5:5 says, "And a certain man was there, which had an infirmity thirty and eight years." The word "certain" is the Greek word *tis*, which indicates *someone certain*; *specific*; and *notable*. This was a man everyone knew very well and was actually still alive at the time John's gospel was written.

He "had an infirmity." The word "had" is again the Greek word *echo*, meaning *to be suppressed or restrained*. This man had been in the restraining grip of an "infirmity" for 38 years. The Greek word for "infirmity" is *astheneia*, and it describes *a person who is frail in health*; *one so physically weak that he is unable to travel*; *one who is feeble, fragile, faint, incapacitated, disabled, or simply in such poor health that it would be unthinkable to transport him*; *one who is shut in or homebound*. It can also mean *to be in financial need*.

John 5:6 says, "When Jesus saw him lie, and knew that he had been now a long time in that case, he saith unto him, Wilt thou be made whole?" The word "saw" in this verse is the Greek is *horao*, which means *to see; to behold; to perceive*. It pictures *a scrutinizing look with the intent to fully examine; to fully view*. It also carries the idea *to experience; to know from personal observation*.

Also notice the word "lie." It is the same Greek word used for "lay" in verse 3 — the word *katakeimai*. In context, it pictures *one who is very sick; lying down; down and out*. When Jesus "saw" (*horao*) this man — when He took a scrutinizing look and fully comprehended his condition — He knew that this man wasn't just lying down physically; he was also lying down on the inside. The man had given up hope and had accepted his circumstances, probably believing things would never change.

Once Jesus diagnosed the man's physical and spiritual state, He moved forward to restore his life. And He desires to do the same thing for you and for those you know who are ready to be made whole.

STUDY QUESTIONS

> Study to shew thyself approved unto God, a workman that needeth not to be ashamed, rightly dividing the word of truth.
> — 2 Timothy 2:15

1. When Jesus shows up in your life, *everything can change*! Take a few moments to chew on the spiritual nourishment in Genesis 18:14; Matthew 19:26; Luke 1:37; and Ephesians 3:20. What resounding truth is the Holy Spirit showing you in these verses that you need to hold tightly to?
2. David had been handpicked and anointed by God to be king of Israel. Yet he endured many trials and troubles before God's promise became a reality. In Psalm 27:13 and 14 (*AMPC*), he said, "[What, what would have become of me] had I not believed that I would see the Lord's goodness in the land of the living! Wait and hope for and expect the Lord; be brave and of good courage and let your heart be stout and enduring. Yes, wait for and hope for and expect the Lord." Knowing that God kept His word to David, how do his words encourage you to trust God and believe that He will be faithful to you?

PRACTICAL APPLICATION

> But be ye doers of the word, and not hearers only, deceiving your own selves.
> — James 1:22

Proverbs 13:12 (*NKJV*) says, "Hope deferred makes the heart sick, but when desire comes, it is a tree of life." The man who had been held captive by sickness for 38 years had lost hope — he was lying down on the inside.

1. How about you? Are you dealing with a lingering sickness? If so, what is it? Take a few moments to describe your situation and surrender it afresh to the Lord.

2. Is your heart sick from prolonged delay to your prayers? How does this lesson encourage you to hold on to the hope that healing is yours through Jesus Christ?

LESSON 3

TOPIC
The Question That Will Change Your Life

SCRIPTURES

1. **John 5:1-6** — After this there was a feast of the Jews; and Jesus went up to Jerusalem. Now there is at Jerusalem by the sheep market a pool, which is called in the Hebrew tongue Bethesda, having five porches. In these lay a great multitude of impotent folk, of blind, halt, withered, waiting for the moving of the water. For an angel went down at a certain season into the pool, and troubled the water: whosoever then first after the troubling of the water stepped in was made whole of whatsoever disease he had. And a certain man was there, which had an infirmity thirty and eight years. When Jesus saw him lie, and knew that he had been now a long time in that case, he saith unto him, Wilt thou be made whole?

GREEK WORDS

1. "sheep market" — προβατικῇ (*probatike*): pictures a sheep gate; a gate where sheep were kept or sold for temple sacrifices, and it was only a short distance from the temple

2. "pool" — κολυμβήθρα (*kolumbethra*): a pool; a highly sophisticated, beautiful, developed place

3. "Bethesda" — **Βηθζαθά** (*Bethzatha*): a house of mercy; a house of grace; a house of goodness
4. "porches" — **στοὰς** (*stoas*): covered porches; covered porticoes; covered colonnades
5. "lay" — **κατάκειμαι** (*katakeimai*): to lie down; pictures things that are piled around
6. "great multitude" — **πλῆθος** (*plethos*): a great number; a multitude
7. "impotent folk" — **ἀσθενέω** (*astheneo*): describes a person who is frail in health; one so physically weak that he is unable to travel; one who is feeble, fragile, faint, incapacitated, disabled, or simply in such poor health that it would be unthinkable to transport him; shut in or homebound; can also mean to be in financial need
8. "blind" — **τυφλός** (*tuphlos*): blind, physically or mentally
9. "halt" — **χωλός** (*cholos*): maimed; deprived of limbs; crippled
10. "withered" — **ξηρός** (*xeros*): deprived of their natural strength; pictures those whose physical limbs are shrunk, wasted, or withered away
11. "waiting" — **ἐκδέχομαι** (*ekdechomai*): from **ἐκ** (*ek*), meaning out, and **δέχομαι** (*dechomai*), meaning welcome; to welcome; to await; to fully expect; to anticipate; pictures looking to the end result or outcome of the waiting; full expectation and anticipation
12. "moving" — **κίνησις** (*kenesis*): stirring; commotion; agitation; fierce moving
13. "went down" — **καταβαίνω** (*katabaino*): to descend, like stepping down a set of stairs
14. "troubled" — **ταράσσω** (*tarasso*): to disturb; to distress; to panic; to deeply trouble; to trouble back and forth; to be deeply disturbed
15. "stepped in" — **ἐμβαίνω** (*embaino*): to step in, as to step into a pool
16. "whole" — **ὑγιής** (*hugies*): healthy; sound; well; whole; fully restored to normal health
17. "disease" — **νόσος** (*nosos*): a terminal condition for which there is no natural cure; in the ancient world, it especially described spirit-induced illnesses; this type of disease held no hope of recuperation; an unalterable, irreversible, incurable condition
18. "he had" — **ἔχω** (*echo*): tense meaning having; also, to be in the embrace of; suppressed; restrained
19. "infirmity" — **ἀσθενεία** (*astheneia*): describes a person who is frail in health; one so physically weak that he is unable to travel; one who is

feeble, fragile, faint, incapacitated, disabled, or simply in such poor health that it would be unthinkable to transport him; shut-in or homebound; can also mean to be in financial need

20. "saw" — ὁράω (*horao*): to see; to behold; to perceive; pictures a scrutinizing look; to look with the intent to examine; to fully view; to experience; to know from personal observation

21. "lie" — κατάκειμαι (*katakeimai*): in context, pictures one who is very sick; lying down; down and out

22. "knew" — γινώσκω (*ginosko*): to know, perceive, or comprehend; to recognize a person or a thing; to acknowledge; to have a full comprehension about a person or thing

23. "had" — ἔχω (*echo*): tense meaning having; also, to be in the embrace of; suppressed; restrained

24. "long time" — πολὺν ἤδη χρόνον (*polun ede chronon*): a long time already in this chronic condition

25. "wilt thou" — Θέλεις (*Theleis*): a form of θέλω (*thelo*), conveying desire, wish, will, or intention

SYNOPSIS

The Pool of Bethesda is located in the old city of Jerusalem. Looking back 2,000 years on this area, one can see that it was thriving with people. As we have also seen, Bethesda was a very beautiful, sophisticated, and luxurious place. It had originally been built for the wealthy and elite, but after they abandoned it, the poor and sick took up occupancy. It was here that Jesus visited a man who had been immobilized by illness for 38 years. To him Christ posed this question that would forever change his life: "Wilt thou be made whole?"

The emphasis of this lesson:

A whole set of ramifications would be set in motion and in place with the paralyzed man's healing and restoration by the power of God. Jesus asked the man an interesting question before He blessed Him. And just as the moment of truth came for that man at the Pool of Bethesda, your moment of truth is on its way. Before Jesus transforms your life, you, too, will need to answer His question: "Do you really want to be healed?"

Bethesda: The Place of Miracles

To understand the setting in which this miracle took place, we need to examine John 5:1 and 2. That passage reads, "After this there was a feast of the Jews; and Jesus went up to Jerusalem. Now there is at Jerusalem by the sheep market a pool, which is called in the Hebrew tongue Bethesda, having five porches."

The words "sheep market" in Greek is the word *probatike*, which actually means *the sheep gate*. It's a literal place you can still visit in Jerusalem today, and there is a pool nearby just as there was in the First Century — the Pool of Bethesda. The word "pool" is the Greek word *kolumbethra*, and it describes *a pool that is highly developed, sophisticated, and very beautiful*. It is the same word used to describe the Pool of Siloam, which was also a highly elaborate and luxurious place nearby.

Originally, the Pool of Bethesda, which went by another name, was built for and occupied by the affluent, highly educated, and wealthy. Over time, however, they abandoned it and it was taken over by the severely sick and the poor. It was these societal rejects who actually nicknamed or renamed the pool "Bethesda," which is the Greek word *Bethzatha*, meaning *a house of mercy; a house of grace; a house of goodness*. Indeed, this was a place where God poured out His mercy, His grace, and His goodness on those who were in dire straits.

A Vast Multitude Lay Beneath Its Porches

We know from research and excavations that Bethesda had two pools: an upper pool, which was 60 feet long, and a lower pool, which was 55 feet in length. It was the upper pool that was covered with five magnificent porches. We learned that the word "porches" is the Greek word *stoas* — a very familiar term that describes *covered porticoes, colonnades, or walkways*. These *stoas* featured beautifully hand-carved columns, mosaics in the pavement, and tile-covered roofs.

Beneath these covered porches "...lay a great multitude of impotent folk, of blind, halt, withered, waiting for the moving of the water" (John 5:3). The word "lay" in this verse is the Greek word *katakeimai* — the same Greek word used to describe Peter's mother-in-law who "lay sick of a fever" (*see* Mark 1:30). Before Jesus healed her, she was incapacitated and unable to function. The same was true of the sick at the Pool of Bethesda.

The Bible says there was a "great multitude" of those that were sick. The words "great multitude" are from the Greek word *plethos*, which means *a great number; a vast multitude*. The truth is, there were so many people lying around the Pool of Bethesda, they looked like sardines in a can — one person lying tightly next to another, appearing almost to be piled one on top of the other!

The Condition of the People Positioned Around the Pool

The first group of people mentioned that were stationed around the pool were "impotent folk," which is the Greek word *astheneo*. This word describes *a person who is frail in health; one so physically weak that he is unable to travel; one who is feeble, fragile, faint, incapacitated, disabled, or simply in such poor health that it would be unthinkable to transport him*. This is the same word we would use to describe a *shut-in* or *someone who is homebound*. It can also mean *to be in financial need*.

These "impotent folk" had been totally sapped of their strength and left financially destitute as a result of their sickness, which is exactly what sickness does. In addition to robbing you of health, it also steals your time, your energy, your peace, your joy, and it adversely affects your relationships.

The "blind" were a second group of people gathered around Bethesda. The word "blind" is the Greek word *tuphlos*, and it means *blind, physically or mentally*. The "halt" were also present. The Greek word for "halt" is *cholos*, and it describes *those who are maimed, deprived of limbs, or crippled*. The "withered" were also gathered. "Withered" is the Greek word *xeros*, meaning *deprived of natural strength*, and it describes those whose physical limbs are shrunk, wasted, or withered away. This describes the condition of the people at the Pool of Bethesda.

They Waited and Believed for a Miracle

The Bible goes on to say they were all "waiting for the moving of the water" (John 5:3). The word "waiting" in this verse is the Greek word *ekdechomai*, and it carries the idea of *fully expecting and fully anticipating*. These people had their eyes fastened on the water, and they were waiting with great anticipation for it to begin moving. The word "moving" in verse 3 is the Greek word *kenesis*, and it describes *a fierce agitation or stirring*.

There was nothing natural about this movement in the water. It was a supernatural signal that God's merciful presence had arrived.

John 5:4 tells us, "An angel went down at a certain season into the pool, and troubled the water...." The word "troubled" is the Greek word *tarasso*, which means *to deeply disturb; to distress; to panic; to deeply trouble*. It denotes *a back and forth motion* that is totally supernatural in origin. When the people witnessed this supernatural sign, they believed that "…whosoever then first after the troubling of the water stepped in was made whole of whatsoever disease he had" (v. 4).

The word "whole" here is the Greek word *hugies*, which means *to be healthy; sound; well; whole; fully restored to normal health*. The sick people at Bethesda believed, *If I can be the first one to get into the water after it begins to move, I'll be fully restored and I'll get my life back!* Each person believed in that case that he would be "made whole of whatsoever disease he had." The word "disease" is the Greek word *nosos*, and it is used throughout the gospels to describe one particular category of sickness: *a terminal condition for which there is no natural cure*. In the ancient world, it especially described *spirit-induced illnesses. This type of disease held no hope of recuperation. It was an unalterable, irreversible, incurable condition.*

Thus, the people at the Pool of Bethesda had permanent conditions for which there was no medical help or cure. Yet they had come to the pool in faith, waiting for the moving of the water with full anticipation that if they were the first one to make it in when it was troubled, they would be made whole.

Jesus Zeroed in on One Particular Man

John 5:5 says, "And a certain man was there, which had an infirmity thirty and eight years." Interestingly, the word "had" in this verse is a form of the Greek word *echo*, which means *to be in the embrace of; suppressed; restrained*. This man had been *suppressed* and *restrained* by his infirmity for nearly four decades, and as a result, his life had been placed on pause.

The word "infirmity" in verse 5 is the Greek word *astheneia*, and it describes *a person who is frail in health; one so physically weak that he is unable to travel; one who is feeble, fragile, faint, incapacitated, disabled, or simply in such poor health that it would be unthinkable to transport him*. It is the same Greek word translated as "impotent folk" in verse 3.

"When Jesus saw him lie, and knew that he had been now a long time in that case, he saith unto him, Wilt thou be made whole?" (John 5:6) The word "saw" here is the Greek word *horao*, which means *to see; to behold; to perceive*. It pictures *a scrutinizing look* and means *to look with the intent to examine; to fully view; to experience; to know from personal observation*.

By using the word *horao*, the writer shows us that Jesus arrived at the Pool of Bethesda and "saw" this man, He took *a deep scrutinizing look at him*. Jesus' full examination revealed that this man was not just lying down physically — he was also lying down on the inside. In fact, the word "lie" in John 5:6 is the Greek word *katakeimai*, which pictures *one who is very sick; one who is down and out*.

The Scripture says Jesus "knew" that the man had been in that condition for a long time (v. 6). The word "knew" is the Greek word *ginosko*, which means *to really know, perceive, or comprehend; to recognize a person or a thing; to acknowledge; to have a full comprehension about a person or thing*.

Jesus Asked the Paralyzed Man a Very Important Question

When Jesus saw and knew the man's condition internally and externally, He asked him an all-important question: "Wilt thou be made whole?" The words "wilt thou" is the Greek word *Theleis* — a form of the word *thelo*, conveying *desire, wish, will, or intention*. In this verse, it describes *a very strong desire* and carries the idea of asking, "What are your intentions?"

The word "whole," the Greek word *hugies*, means *healthy; sound; fully restored to normal health*. When Jesus asked the man, "Wilt thou be made whole?" He was, in effect, saying, "Do you really intend to be fully restored to normal health? Do you want to stay the way you are, or do you strongly desire to have your life back again?"

Although it may seem strange to ask such a question of a sick man who was waiting to receive his healing, it really wasn't strange at all. Jesus knew that once He healed this man, radical changes would be brought about in his life. He wanted the man to count the costs and be absolutely sure he was ready and willing to embrace those changes.

Jesus is asking you the same question today: "Do you really want to be made well?" In other words, "Do you intend to stay where you are, or do you really want your life back? What are your intentions?" Realize that being made whole will bring about some drastic changes that will require some adjustments in your life. We will focus more on this in the next two lessons.

STUDY QUESTIONS

> Study to shew thyself approved unto God, a workman that needeth not to be ashamed, rightly dividing the word of truth.
> — 2 Timothy 2:15

Waiting is a major part of life, and *how* we wait is very important. The people around the Pool of Bethesda were waiting for the water to be supernaturally agitated. They had a full expectation and anticipation of God showing up at any moment to bring powerful, positive change.

1. How about you? On a scale of one to ten (one being the lowest and ten being the highest), how would you rate your level of anticipation and expectancy for God to bring positive change in your life?
2. If your expectation is low, what do you think needs to happen in your life to bring it up?
3. Take a few moments to meditate on Isaiah 30:18 (*AMPC*): "Therefore the Lord [earnestly] waits [expecting, looking, and longing] to be gracious to you; and therefore He lifts Himself up, that He may have mercy on you and how loving-kindness to you. For the Lord is a God of justice. Blessed (happy, fortunate, to be envied) are all those who [earnestly] wait for Him [for His victory, His favor, His love, His peace, His joy, and His matchless unbroken companionship]!" What is the Holy Spirit speaking to you through this amazing promise?

PRACTICAL APPLICATION

> But be ye doers of the word, and not hearers only, deceiving your own selves.
> — James 1:22

1. Do you know someone who has been immobilized by illness for a prolonged period of time — he wants to be healed but has yet to experience Christ's supernatural touch? Who is it and what is he walking through?

2. In light of what the Holy Spirit is teaching you in these lessons, what can you share with that person to strengthen his faith and revive his hope of receiving healing?
3. In what specific way can you pray for that individual and minister God's healing power?

LESSON 4

TOPIC
The Ramifications of Total Healing in Your Life

SCRIPTURES
1. **John 5:1-9** — After this there was a feast of the Jews; and Jesus went up to Jerusalem. Now there is at Jerusalem by the sheep market a pool, which is called in the Hebrew tongue Bethesda, having five porches. In these lay a great multitude of impotent folk, of blind, halt, withered, waiting for the moving of the water. For an angel went down at a certain season into the pool, and troubled the water: whosoever then first after the troubling of the water stepped in was made whole of whatsoever disease he had. And a certain man was there, which had an infirmity thirty and eight years. When Jesus saw him lie, and knew that he had been now a long time in that case, he saith unto him, Wilt thou be made whole? The impotent man answered him, Sir, I have no man, when the water is troubled, to put me into the pool: but while I am coming, another steppeth down before me. Jesus saith unto him, Rise, take up thy bed, and walk. And immediately the man was made whole, and took up his bed, and walked: and on the same day was the sabbath.

GREEK WORDS
1. "sheep market" — προβατικῇ (*probatike*): pictures a sheep gate; a gate where sheep were kept or sold for temple sacrifices, and it was only a short distance from the temple

2. "pool" — κολυμβήθρα (*kolumbethra*): a pool; a highly sophisticated, beautiful, developed place
3. "Bethesda" — Βηθζαθά (*Bethzatha*): a house of mercy; a house of grace; a house of goodness
4. "porches" — στοὰς (*stoas*): covered porches; covered porticoes; covered colonnades
5. "lay" — κατάκειμαι (*katakeimai*): to lie down; pictures things that are piled around
6. "great multitude" — πλῆθος (*plethos*): a great number; a multitude
7. "impotent folk" — ἀσθενέω (*astheneo*): describes a person who is frail in health; one so physically weak that he is unable to travel; one who is feeble, fragile, faint, incapacitated, disabled, or simply in such poor health that it would be unthinkable to transport him; shut-in or homebound; can also mean to be in financial need
8. "blind" — τυφλός (*tuphlos*): blind, physically or mentally
9. "halt" — χωλός (*cholos*): maimed; deprived of limbs; crippled
10. "withered" — ξηρός (*xeros*): deprived of their natural strength; physical limbs are shrunk, wasted, withered away
11. "waiting" — ἐκδέχομαι (*ekdechomai*): from ἐκ (ek), meaning out, and δέχομαι, meaning welcome; to welcome; to await; to fully expect; to anticipate; pictures looking to the end-result or outcome of the waiting; full expectation and anticipation
12. "moving" — κίνησις (*kenesis*): stirring; commotion; agitation; fierce moving
13. "went down" — καταβαίνω (*katabaino*): to descend, like stepping down a set of stairs
14. "troubled" — ταράσσω (*tarasso*): to disturb; to distress; to panic; to deeply trouble; to trouble back and forth; to be deeply disturbed
15. "stepped in" — ἐμβαίνω (*embaino*): to step in, as to step into a pool
16. "whole" — ὑγιής (*hugies*): healthy; sound; well; whole; fully restored to normal health
17. "disease" — νόσος (nosos): a terminal condition for which there is no natural cure; in the ancient world, it especially described spirit-induced illnesses; this type of disease held no hope of recuperation; an unalterable, irreversible, incurable condition
18. "he had" — ἔχω (*echo*): tense meaning having; also, to be in the embrace of; suppressed; restrained

19. "certain" — τις (*tis*): certain; specific; notable
20. "infirmity" — ἀσθενείᾳ (*astheneia*): describes a person who is frail in health; one so physically weak that he is unable to travel; one who is feeble, fragile, faint, incapacitated, disabled, or simply in such poor health that it would be unthinkable to transport him; shut-in or homebound; can also mean to be in financial need
21. "saw" — ὁράω (*horao*): to see; to behold; to perceive; pictures a scrutinizing look; to look with the intent to examine; to fully view; to experience; to know from personal observation
22. "lie" — κατάκειμαι (*katakeimai*): in context, pictures one who is very sick; lying down; down and out
23. "knew" — γινώσκω (*ginosko*): to know, perceive, or comprehend; to recognize a person or a thing; to acknowledge; to have a full comprehension about a person or thing
24. "had" — ἔχω (*echo*): tense meaning having; also, to be in the embrace of; suppressed; restrained
25. "long time" — πολὺν ἤδη χρόνον (*polun ede chronon*): a long time already in this chronic condition
26. "wilt thou" — Θέλεις (*Theleis*): a form of θέλω (thelo), conveying desire, wish, will, or intention
27. "impotent man" — ἀσθενείᾳ (*astheneia*): describes a person who is frail in health; one so physically weak that he is unable to travel; one who is feeble, fragile, faint, incapacitated, disabled, or simply in such poor health that it would be unthinkable to transport him; shut-in or homebound; can also mean to be in financial need
28. "Sir" — Κύριε (*Kurie*): Lord; supreme master
29. "put me into" — βάλλω (*ballo*): to cast; to hurl
30. "Rise" — ἐγείρω (*egeiro*): the tense is a command; to rise, even to rise from the dead
31. "take up" — αἴρω (*airo*): to take up; to physically lift
32. "bed" — κράβαττος (*krabattos*): mattress; a pallet for a poor man
33. "walk" — περιπατέω (*peripateo*): to walk around
34. "immediately" — εὐθέως (*eutheos*): immediately; without delay
35. "walked" — περιπατέω (*peripateo*): to walk around

SYNOPSIS

During the First Century, the Pool of Bethesda was overflowing with sick people waiting for their opportunity to receive healing. One man in particular had been there for 38 years. In faith, he had left the familiar surroundings of his home in hopes of getting his life back. Many miracles had taken place since his arrival at the Pool — so many that he could have written a book on them. When Jesus arrived, He took a scrutinizing look at this man and asked him, "Wilt thou be made whole?" Today, He is asking you this same question. "Do you really want to change? Are you ready to embrace all that comes with being made whole and released from your present condition?"

The emphasis of this lesson:

When Jesus brings healing and transformation to our lives, the effects are far-reaching. So as you ask Him to move in your life, consider the full ramifications of the changes that will come with total restoration.

What We've Discovered So Far

In keeping with Jewish customs, Jesus went up to Jerusalem to observe one of the festivals (*see* John 5:1). "Now there is at Jerusalem by the sheep market a pool, which is called in the Hebrew tongue Bethesda, having five porches" (John 5:2).

The phrase "sheep market" is the Greek word *probatike*. It actually describes the *sheep gate*, not the sheep market. It was *the place near the temple where sheep were kept and sold for temple sacrifices.*

Just beyond the sheep gate was a "pool" called Bethesda. The word "pool" is the Greek word *kolumbethra*, and it describes *a highly sophisticated, beautifully developed place.* This wasn't a low-level pool of water. It was a luxurious pool with five "porches."

The word "porches" is the Greek word *stoas*. It describes *covered colonnades and covered porticoes.* These elaborate covered walkways could be seen throughout the Greek and Roman world, and they featured hand-carved columns, exquisite marble, detailed mosaics, and roofs made of terracotta tiles.

Bethesda was originally built for the wealthy, elite, and intelligentsia of the day. It was so large that it had not one, but *five* porches in all, indicating that an immense amount of money had been invested in its construction. Archaeological research confirms that there were two pools at Bethesda: an upper pool that was 60 feet in length and a lower pool that was 55 feet long. The upper pool was the one with five porches.

The original name of the pool was not Bethesda. After the pool had been vacated by the affluent, the poor and the sick took up residency. They nicknamed the pool "Bethesda," which in Greek means *the house of mercy, the house of grace,* or *the house of goodness*. The sick called it "Bethesda," as it was a place where God poured out His grace, mercy, and goodness.

The people at Bethesda were extremely sick. John 5:3 says, "In these [five porches] lay a great multitude of impotent folk, of blind, halt, withered, waiting for the moving of the water." The word "lay" is the Greek word *katakeimai,* and it describes *those that are down and out, incapacitated, and their life is on pause*. The Bible says there was a "great multitude" that lay there. The words "great multitude" is from the Greek word *plethos,* meaning *a great number; a vast multitude*.

There were many "impotent folk" present. The phrase "impotent folk" is the Greek word *astheneo,* and it describes *a person who is frail in health; one so physically weak that he is unable to travel; one who is feeble, fragile, faint, incapacitated, disabled, or simply in such poor health that it would be unthinkable to transport him*. This is the same Greek word for *a shut-in* or *one that is homebound*.

The word *astheneo,* translated here as "impotent folk," can also refer to *a person in financial need*. As we've noted, sickness is a thief. It steals your health, your strength, your peace, your joy, and your finances. It robs you of your time, your attention, and negatively impacts your relationships. The sick people at Bethesda had been stolen from on many levels.

The "blind," the "halt," and the "withered" were all there. The word "blind" is the Greek word *tuphlos,* and it describes *those who are blind, physically or mentally*. The word "halt" is the Greek word *cholos,* which refers to *the maimed; those deprived of limbs;* and *the crippled*. And the word "withered" is from the Greek word *xeros,* which means *deprived of natural strength*. These were people whose physical limbs had *shrunk, been wasted,* or *withered away*. The term *xeros* is where we get the word *zero*. The "withered" were considered to be the big "zeros" of society.

They were all "waiting for the moving of the water." The Greek word for "waiting" in this verse is *ekdechomai*, and it basically describes *a full anticipation and full expectation*. As the eyes of the sick were fixated on the water, waiting for it to move, they fully expected a positive end-result.

The word "moving" here is the Greek word *kenesis*, and it describes *a fierce stirring or agitation; a commotion*. This was not a natural movement of water but a supernatural movement.

"An angel went down...and troubled the water" (John 5:4). The source of the supernatural stirring was believed to be the work of an angel. The word "troubled" in verse 4 is the Greek word *tarasso*, which means *to deeply disturb; to distress; to panic; to trouble back and forth*. Again, there was nothing natural about the water's movement. It was not the rippling effect of the wind on the water's surface. This troubling of the water was a supernatural swirling in a fierce circular fashion.

The first one in was made "whole." The Bible says, "...Whosoever then first after the troubling of the water stepped in was made whole of whatsoever disease he had" (John 5:4). The word "whole" is again the Greek word *hugies*, which means *healthy; sound; well; whole; fully restored to normal health*. The sick beside the pool believed that the troubling of the water was the signal that God's healing power was available in that moment. They trusted that if they were the first to enter the water as it was being stirred, they would be totally restored to health and get their life back.

Their lives had been suppressed by sickness. Looking again at John 5:4, it tells us that each sick person believed he would be "made whole of whatsoever disease he had." The word "had" is a form of the Greek word *echo*, which means *to be in the embrace of; to suppress; to restrain*. The lives of these sick people had been suppressed and restrained by sickness. More than anything, they wanted their lives back — they wanted to be made "whole."

One man had been at Bethesda for 38 years. John 5:5 says, "And a certain man was there, which had an infirmity thirty and eight years." The word "had" is a form of the Greek word *echo* in verse 4. It means this man's life had been *restrained*, or *put on pause*, for nearly four decades by this infirmity. The word "infirmity" is the Greek word *astheneia*, and it describes people who are frail in health and so physically weak that *they are unable to travel*, and *they are feeble, fragile, faint, incapacitated, and disabled*. This is a picture of this man and the condition he had endured for 38 years.

Sickness had affected every area of his life and had left him financially depleted.

He had come to Bethesda believing he would be healed. This man had heard of Bethesda — the place where God's *mercy, grace,* and *goodness* were being poured out. In faith, he had left the familiar surroundings of his home and the care of family members with the hopes of being made whole. Although he was expecting and anticipating a miracle from God, he only witnessed the healing of others. Still crippled and unchanged after 38 years, he had given up hope.

Jesus fully perceived this man's condition. John 5:6 says, "When Jesus saw him lie, and knew that he had been now a long time in that case, he saith unto him, Wilt thou be made whole?" The word "saw" in this verse is the Greek word *horao*, which means *to see; to behold; to perceive.* It pictures *a scrutinizing look with the intent to fully examine and fully view,* and as a result, *to fully comprehend.*

When Jesus "saw" this man, He didn't just take a quick glance. He stopped and focused His eyes on him and fully assessed his condition — both inside and out. Jesus sees you in the same way. He is able to discern the complete details of what is going on with you *internally* as well as *externally.* The man at Bethesda was not just lying down physically; he was also lying down spiritually. That is, he had given up hope inwardly.

Jesus asked, "Wilt thou be made whole?" The phrase "wilt thou" is the Greek word *Theleis,* a form of the word *thelo* that conveys *desire, wish, will,* or *intention.* In this verse, "Wilt thou be made whole" means, "Do you really intend to be made whole? What are your intentions?"

Again, the word "whole" is the Greek word *hugies,* which means *to be fully restored to normal health* or *to get one's life back.* Jesus was asking this man, "Do you want to stay the way you are, or do you want to get your life back again?"

This was a huge question with great ramifications. For this man to be made whole — for him to get his life back again — it meant several things would need to change. First, he would have to leave the Pool of Bethesda. Second, he would have to find new friends; all of the sick people around the pool he had been in relationship with would be out of the picture. Third, he would need to get a job and start working. Since he hadn't worked in 38 years, he would probably need to receive some kind of education or training. Last, the man would also need to begin feeding and caring for himself.

How Did the Sick Man Respond to Jesus?

John 5:7 says, "The impotent man answered him, Sir, I have no man, when the water is troubled, to put me into the pool: but while I am coming, another steppeth down before me." First, notice that the man called Jesus "Sir." The word "Sir" is the Greek word *Kurie*, which means *Lord; supreme master*. So he acknowledged the *lordship* of Jesus.

He then said, "I have no one." The word "no" is the Greek word *ouk*, and by using this word, it emphatically communicated, "I don't have anyone to help me." That is often how people respond when someone asks them if they want to change. They immediately shift the focus off themselves and onto others. It is as if they are saying, "Well, I would change if my spouse would help," or "if my boss would act differently," or "if others would come to my aid." That is how this man responded.

He told Jesus, "I have no man, when the water is troubled, to put me into the pool...." The phrase "put me into" is the Greek word *ballo*, which means *to cast; to hurl*. Essentially, this man wanted to get into the water first, but he never made it in because someone always got in before him.

Jesus Commanded the Man To Get Up

After the man offered his take on the situation, Jesus looked at him and said, "Rise, take up thy bed, and walk..." (John 5:8). The word "rise" is the Greek word *egeiro*, and it is *a very strong command to rise, even to rise from the dead*. This is the same word that is often used in the New Testament to describe the *act of resurrection*.

The word "bed" is the Greek word *krabattos*, and it describes *a mattress or a pallet for a poor man*. Essentially, Jesus commanded this man to get up off of his affliction, pick his affliction up, and walk. The word "walk" in this verse is the Greek word *peripateo*, which means *to walk around*. This word tells us that Jesus wasn't just telling him to take a few steps; He was telling him to get up and get moving. He was calling this man out of His infirmity and into wholeness.

In the same way, Jesus is calling you *to get up and get moving*. He wants you to, by faith, *rise* from the debilitating situation you have been in and start moving forward into His plan for your life.

STUDY QUESTIONS

> Study to shew thyself approved unto God, a workman that needeth not to be ashamed, rightly dividing the word of truth.
> — 2 Timothy 2:15

1. When Jesus asked the sick man at Bethesda if he really wanted to be healed, the man didn't answer Jesus' question directly. Instead, he shifted the focus onto others. How do you normally respond when the Holy Spirit asks you a direct question? Is there any value in casting blame?
2. Isaiah 60:1 (*AMPC*) says, "Arise [from the depression and prostration in which circumstances have kept you—rise to a new life]! Shine (be radiant with the glory of the Lord), for your light has come, and the glory of the Lord has risen upon you!" What is the Lord speaking to you through this command in light of your current situation?

PRACTICAL APPLICATION

> But be ye doers of the word, and not hearers only, deceiving your own selves.
> — James 1:22

1. Think for a moment. What is the most difficult situation you are facing right now — physically, mentally, emotionally, vocationally, or relationally — that you desperately need Jesus to touch and heal?
2. If Jesus were to radically heal and transform this area of your life, what are some of the changes that would take place and be required of you once He brought it about? (Consider what the man at the Pool of Bethesda needed to change. If you're not sure, take a moment to pray and ask the Holy Spirit to reveal things to you.)
3. Are you sure you want to be healed? Are you ready and willing to embrace all the changes that are needed to experience this transformation? This is a question you need to answer honestly as you seek the Lord.

LESSON 5

TOPIC
What if Others Don't Rejoice When You Change?

SCRIPTURES

1. **John 5:1-15** — After this there was a feast of the Jews; and Jesus went up to Jerusalem. Now there is at Jerusalem by the sheep market a pool, which is called in the Hebrew tongue Bethesda, having five porches. In these lay a great multitude of impotent folk, of blind, halt, withered, waiting for the moving of the water. For an angel went down at a certain season into the pool, and troubled the water: whosoever then first after the troubling of the water stepped in was made whole of whatsoever disease he had. And a certain man was there, which had an infirmity thirty and eight years. When Jesus saw him lie, and knew that he had been now a long time in that case, he saith unto him, Wilt thou be made whole? The impotent man answered him, Sir, I have no man, when the water is troubled, to put me into the pool: but while I am coming, another steppeth down before me. Jesus saith unto him, Rise, take up thy bed, and walk. And immediately the man was made whole, and took up his bed, and walked: and on the same day was the sabbath. The Jews therefore said unto him that was cured, It is the sabbath day: it is not lawful for thee to carry thy bed. He answered them, He that made me whole, the same said unto me, Take up thy bed, and walk. Then asked they him, What man is that which said unto thee, Take up thy bed, and walk? And he that was healed wist not who it was: for Jesus had conveyed himself away, a multitude being in that place. Afterward Jesus findeth him in the temple, and said unto him, Behold, thou art made whole: sin no more, lest a worse thing come unto thee. The man departed, and told the Jews that it was Jesus, which had made him whole.

GREEK WORDS

1. "impotent man" — ἀσθενείᾳ (*astheneia*): describes a person who is frail in health; one so physically weak that he is unable to travel; one

who is feeble, fragile, faint, incapacitated, disabled, or simply in such poor health that it would be unthinkable to transport him; shut-in or homebound; can also mean to be in financial need

2. "Sir" — Κύριε (*Kurie*): Lord; supreme master
3. "put me into" — βάλλω (*ballo*): to cast; to hurl
4. "Rise" — ἐγείρω (*egeiro*): the tense is a command; to rise, even to rise from the dead
5. "take up" — αἴρω (*airo*): to take up; to physically lift
6. "bed" — κράβαττος (*krabattos*): mattress; a pallet for a poor man
7. "walk" — περιπατέω (*peripateo*): to walk around
8. "immediately" — εὐθέως (*eutheos*): immediately; without delay
9. "whole" — ὑγιής (*hugies*): healthy; sound; well; whole; fully restored to normal health
10. "walked" — περιπατέω (*peripateo*): to walk around
11. "cured" — θεραπεύω (*therapeuo*): therapy; a healing touch that requires corresponding actions
12. "carry" — αἴρω (*airo*): to take up; to physically lift
13. "healed" — ἰάομαι (*iaomai*): to cure; to be doctored; pictures a healing power that progressively reverses a condition; mostly denoted healing that came to pass over a period of time
14. "findeth" — εὑρίσκω (*heurisko*): to find or to discover; pictures a discovery made due to an intense investigation
15. "behold" — ὁράω (*horao*): in this context, to see; to comprehend; to perceive; to understand
16. "worse thing" — χείρων (*cheiron*): worse; more severe
17. "made" — ποιέω (*poieo*): to do; to creatively do; same root for the word "poet"

SYNOPSIS

During the days of Jesus, the Pool of Bethesda was an impressive sight to see. Its remnants can still be viewed today just north of the temple mount near the ruins of the basilica of St. Anne. The Jews believed Bethesda was a place of supernatural healing — it was *the house of God's mercy, grace, and goodness*. It was there that Jesus encountered a man who had been bound by infirmity for 38 years — and Jesus completely restored this man to health. Although many rejoiced over this man's miracle, there were some who were outraged, and they quickly made their opinions known.

The emphasis of this lesson:
Not everyone was happy for the man who had been healed by Jesus at Bethesda, and not everyone will be happy for you when God does a work in your life. But don't let that keep you from believing for and receiving the miracle He has waiting.

Jesus Fully Investigated the Man at Bethesda

John 5:6 says, "When Jesus saw him [the sick man] lie, and knew that he had been now a long time in that case, he saith unto him, Wilt thou be made whole?" As we have seen in previous lessons, the word "saw" is the Greek word *horao*, which means *to see; to behold; to perceive.* It pictures *a scrutinizing look,* and it means *to look with the intent to fully examine and fully view,* and as a result, *to fully comprehend.*

When Jesus looked at this sick man, He fixed His eyes on him to study and fully investigate him and his situation. Consequently, He was able to see and comprehend the man's condition internally as well externally. It is the same thing Jesus does when He looks at and studies you.

Scripture says that Jesus saw him "lie," which means He could see that the man was not just lying down physically — he was also lying down in his soul and spirit. His heart had lost hope that he would ever be healed, and his outward posture reflected his inward despair.

Jesus Then Asked an All-Important Question

"Wilt thou be made whole?" He asked. The phrase "wilt thou" is the Greek word *Theleis,* which is a form of the word *thelo,* and it conveys *desire, wish, will,* or *intention.* The word "whole" is the Greek word *hugies,* which means *healthy; sound; fully restored to normal health.* In this verse, Jesus' question "Wilt thou be made whole" was the equivalent of His saying, "What is your intention? Do you really want to be fully restored to health? Do you really want your life back?"

This question may seem strange to ask someone who had been waiting 38 years to receive his healing, but it was actually quite valid. For nearly four decades this man didn't have a job, nor did he have to feed or take care of himself. All his friends were sick people, and the subject that filled their conversations was sickness. *His infirmity had become his identity.*

Jesus knew that if He healed this man, everything in his life would need to change. His thinking would have to change. His place of residence and those he hung out with would have to change. He would also need to get a job and begin feeding and caring for himself. Having gainful employment would likely require vocational training and possibly going back to school. Thus, being healed was not just a matter of feeling better — it was a matter of undergoing major life changes.

The same is true for you. If Jesus releases His life-transforming power in your life, it is going to bring radical changes. As He asked the man at Bethesda, He is also asking you today: "Are you sure you want to be healed? Are you ready and willing to embrace the life change that will come about as a result?" This is a question you really need to answer honestly as you seek the Lord.

Jesus Countered the Impotent Man's Response

After Jesus asked His direct question, John 5:7 says, "The impotent man answered him, Sir, I have no man, when the water is troubled, to put me into the pool: but while I am coming, another steppeth down before me."

First, notice the man addressed Jesus as "Sir." This is the Greek word *Kurie*, which is a form of the word *Kurios*, meaning *Lord* or *supreme master*. This man acknowledged the supreme authority of Jesus and recognized that He was in control. If you are going to be healed, you, too, must acknowledge the supreme authority of Jesus and be willing to do whatever He tells you to do.

Upon hearing the man's response, "Jesus saith unto him, Rise, take up thy bed, and walk" (John 5:8). The word "rise" is the Greek word *egeiro*, and *the tense is a command*. It means *to rise, even to rise from the dead*. When Jesus commanded this man to "rise," it was the equivalent of a resurrection. He had been restrained by affliction for 38 years, and now his moment of restoration had arrived.

Jesus then said, "Take up thy bed." The phrase "take up" is the Greek word *airo*, which means *to take up; to physically lift*. Jesus commanded this man to *physically lift* his "bed" after he had been bedridden for nearly four decades. The word "bed" is the Greek word *krabattos*, and it describes *a mattress or a pallet for a poor man.*

To all this, Jesus added the command, "Walk." In Greek, this word "walk" is the word *peripateo*, and it means *to walk around.* By using this word, we know that Jesus didn't just ask the man to take a few steps. He told him *to get up and get moving.*

The Man's Obedience Yielded Results

What would have happened if this man had said, "Rise, Lord? What do you mean?" or, "Walk, Lord? I can barely move, much less walk. I've been lying on this dilapidated bed for years, and my body is totally void of strength. I just can't do what You're asking me." If this man would have responded in this way, he would have remained at the Pool of Bethesda for the rest of his life. But he didn't. Instead, he acknowledged Jesus' lordship and did what He said to do.

What happened when the man obeyed Jesus' words? John 5:9 says, "And immediately the man was made whole, and took up his bed, and walked: and on the same day was the sabbath." The word "immediately" is the Greek word *eutheos*, and it means *immediately; without delay*, and the word "whole" is once again the Greek word *hugies*, which means *healthy; fully restored to normal health.* It carries *the idea of getting one's life back.*

As instructed, the man then "took up his bed." The words "took up" is the same Greek word that is translated "take up" in verse 11. It is the word *airo*, meaning *to take up; to physically lift.* This man *picked up* his "bed"— the Greek word *krabattos*, which describes *the mattress or pallet for a poor man* — and he *walked*! The word "walked" is the Greek word *peripateo*, meaning *to walk around.* When Jesus spoke the word of healing, this man believed it, received it, and began walking out God's promises.

Not Everyone Rejoiced at His Healing

Jesus' visit to the Pool of Bethesda and the healing of the man who had been restrained and suppressed by infirmity for 38 years all took place on the Sabbath. Consequently, "The Jews therefore said unto him that was cured, It is the sabbath day: it is not lawful for thee to carry thy bed" (John 5:10). No work was to be done on the Sabbath, and since it took effort for this man to carry his bed, the Jewish leaders saw that as work. "You're breaking the law," they snarled. "Stop it! Stop it now!"

But that wasn't all the man did. The religious leaders had created a rule stating that a person could only walk a short distance on the Sabbath, and this man had been walking around carrying his bed — just as Jesus had told him — for quite some time. Apparently, he had exceeded his allotted walking quota for the Sabbath, and the religious leaders called him on it.

Imagine that. This man that had been sick for 38 years had finally received his miracle, and the religious leaders couldn't rejoice in what God had done. Basically, they told him, "This is the Sabbath. What do you mean by carrying your bed? What do you mean by walking more than you are permitted? You're breaking the rules. Today is just not a good time for you to change. Get back on your bed and be still."

Realize that when God touches your life, not everyone will rejoice with you, either. Some people have become accustomed to you as a broken, sick individual, and they will not like you in your newly restored state. And as a result of their not knowing how to relate to you, they will attempt to put you back on your "sickbed." That is what these religious leaders did to the man at Bethesda.

Two Types of Healing Were on Display

The Bible goes on to say, "He [the man who had been healed] answered them, He that made me whole, the same said unto me, Take up thy bed, and walk. Then asked they him, What man is that which said unto thee, Take up thy bed, and walk? And he that was healed wist not who it was: for Jesus had conveyed himself away, a multitude being in that place" (John 5:11-13).

The word "healed" in verse 13 is the Greek word *iaomai*, and it means *to cure; to be doctored*. It pictures *a healing power that progressively reverses a condition*, and it mostly denoted *healing that came to pass over a period of time*. By using the word *iaomai* in this verse, the Holy Spirit is telling us that the longer this man walked around, the stronger he became. He was progressively healed.

Interestingly, the Greek word for "healed" (*iaomai*) in verse 13 is different than the word for "cured" in verse 10. The Greek word for "cured" is *therapeuo*, and it is where we get the word *therapy*. It describes *a healing touch that requires corresponding actions*. The word *therapeuo* is the primary word used in the gospels to describe the healing ministry of Jesus — a healing power that operates when someone cooperates in faith with Him.

Think about it. When Jesus came across a man with a withered hand, He told him *to stretch forth his hand*. Likewise, when He met someone who was lame — like the man at the Pool of Bethesda — He told him *to rise up and walk*. Whatever the situation, Jesus required the sick person to cooperate with the healing process by carrying out specific actions. He "therapied" them, and their obedience released the *therapeuo* power of Jesus.

Jesus Followed Up on the Man He Healed

After the religious leaders had completed their interrogation of the man who was healed at Bethesda, the Bible says, "Jesus findeth him in the temple, and said unto him, Behold, thou art made whole: sin no more, lest a worse thing come unto thee" (John 5:14).

First of all, notice the Scripture says Jesus "findeth" him in the temple. This word "findeth" is the Greek word *heurisko*, and it means *to find or to discover*. It pictures *a discovery made due to an intense investigation*. Jesus didn't just heal the man and leave; He followed up on him. He took the time to search him out and investigate how he was doing. He desires to do the same thing in your life. If you will listen to Him, He will walk beside you and continue to instruct you on what to do.

That's what Jesus did for this man. He told him, "Behold, thou art made whole...." The word "behold" is the Greek word *horao*, and in this context, it means *to see; to comprehend; to perceive; to understand*. Jesus wanted the man to be alert and understand that he had been made "whole" — the Greek word *hugies*, meaning *healthy; sound; fully restored to normal health*.

Jesus told him, "Look, I've given you your life back — you're completely healthy. Don't sin anymore, or something worse will come on you." This implies that the man's original sickness had come on him as a result of something he did — it may have been wrong thinking, wrong believing, or wrong behavior.

Whatever the case, Jesus told him not to repeat the same mistakes he had made earlier in his life or a "worse thing" would come on him. The words "worse thing" is the Greek word *cheiron*, and it describes *something worse or more severe*. To avoid a relapse, this man was to take his healing seriously and do whatever he needed to do to keep from falling back into old sin patterns.

John 5:15 goes on to say, "The man departed, and told the Jews that it was Jesus, which had made him whole." The word "made" is the Greek word *poieo*, which is the same root for the word "poet," and it always carries the idea of *doing something creatively*. That is what Jesus did — He creatively restored this man and gave him back his life. If you will obey God and do what He says to do, He will creatively give you your life back too.

STUDY QUESTIONS

Study to shew thyself approved unto God, a workman that needeth
not to be ashamed, rightly dividing the word of truth.
— 2 Timothy 2:15

1. Traditions can be a wonderful thing, but they can also become detrimental to your walk with God if they get out of balance. The lives of the Pharisees are a perfect example of this. Carefully read Jesus' words in Matthew 15:1-9 and explain how tradition can become deadly. (Also *consider* Mark 7:1-13).
2. Is there an area of your life where you are imitating the Pharisees with regard to traditions? If so, where? What specific actions do you know you need to take to make things right? (*Consider* Colossians 2:8; 2 Timothy 3:15,16.)

PRACTICAL APPLICATION

But be ye doers of the word, and not hearers only,
deceiving your own selves.
— James 1:22

1. Your outward man is a reflection (or picture) of your inner man. If someone were to look at your physical appearance and posture, what might they determine about the true condition of your soul and spirit?
2. The man at the Pool of Bethesda honored Jesus and recognized Him as *Lord*. Are you honoring Jesus as *Supreme Master* and the One who is in ultimate control of your life? If so, how? If you haven't, take a moment to repent and ask Him to forgive you. Then do what you need to do to make things right.
3. Has your life recently been touched by God in the form of a healing, a promotion, or another type of breakthrough? Describe what has taken place.

4. Is there someone who is not happy with how God has blessed you and transformed your life? If so, how does this lesson help you see your situation and the people around you more accurately?

A Prayer To Receive Salvation

If you've never received Jesus as your Savior and Lord, now is the time for you to experience the new life Jesus wants to give you! To receive God's gift of salvation that can be obtained through Jesus alone, pray this prayer from your heart:

Jesus, I repent of my sin and receive You as my Savior and Lord. Wash away my sin with Your precious blood and make me completely new. I thank You that my sin is removed, and Satan no longer has any right to lay claim on me. Through Your empowering grace, I faithfully promise that I will serve You as my Lord for the rest of my life.

If you just prayed this prayer of salvation, you are born again! You are a brand-new creation in Christ! Would you please let us know of your decision by going to **renner.org/salvation**? We would love to connect with you and pray for you as you begin your new life in Christ.

Scriptures for further study: John 3:16; John 14:6; Acts 4:12; Ephesians 1:7; Hebrews 10:19,20; 1 Peter 1:18,19; Romans 10:9,10; Colossians 1:13; 2 Corinthians 5:17; Romans 6:4; 1 Peter 1:3

CLAIM YOUR FREE RESOURCE!

As a way of introducing you further to the teaching ministry of Rick Renner, we would like to send you FREE of charge his teaching, "How To Receive a Miraculous Touch From God" on CD or as an MP3 download.

In His earthly ministry, Jesus commonly healed *all* who were sick of *all* their diseases. In this profound message, learn about the manifold dimensions of Christ's wisdom, goodness, power, and love toward all humanity who came to Him in faith with their needs.

☑ YES, I want to receive Rick Renner's monthly teaching letter!

Simply scan the QR code to claim this resource or go to:
renner.org/claim-your-free-offer

WITH US!

renner.org

facebook.com/rickrenner • facebook.com/rennerdenise
youtube.com/rennerministries • youtube.com/deniserenner
instagram.com/rickrrenner • instagram.com/rennerministries_
instagram.com/rennerdenise

www.ingramcontent.com/pod-product-compliance
Lightning Source LLC
Chambersburg PA
CBHW071649040426
42452CB00009B/1818